The
Focused
LIFE

26
Weekly
Devotionals

Phil Stern

Table of Contents

Acknowledgments

A project like this takes talented people. Two of those people who have been an incredible help and made this book possible are: Mike Hodge and Joel Funkhouser.

Mike did the editing and layout work and spent more than the required time because of his heart for excellence. Thank you Mike, you are the best!

Joel designed and produced the cover. Joel is talented and very willing to give his energy and time to helping someone make their project a dream come true. You are a true friend Joel.

Jess Wade owns Jess Wade Photography. Her photography skills made the photo on the cover possible. Thank you Jess for such great work!

The photo on the front is my daughter Joy. This came from one of her graduation pictures and was exactly what we needed for the project. Thank you Joy for allowing us to use this awesome picture (love your eyes)!

For all the people you have poured into my life with the many truths that are in these devotionals, I thank you so much.

Book Cover Design
Enspire Media – www.enspiremedia.com

Cover Photo
Jess Wade Photography – St. Louis, MO

Editor and layout
Michael D. Hodge – Mike@michaeldhodge.com

Broken Focus

Focus is so important in our life, home and career. It keeps us on track, determined and energized. When we focus, we continue to have clear vision for the future. When focus is broken, it stops momentum and we see everything through dull, blurred eyes. Here are some leaders of the past who lost their focus:

- **King Solomon was focused** when he began his reign and was blessed by God. **His focus was broken** by 700 wives who turned his heart away from God. (Can't imagine that 700 wives would distract a guy.)
- When **Alexander the Great had Focus** and vision, he conquered the known world. **When he lost focus**, he couldn't conquer a liquor bottle.
- When **David was focused**, he conquered Goliath. When he allowed that **focus to be broken**, he couldn't conquer his lust for Bathsheba.

Broken Focus

- When **Samson had focus,** he won every battle. When **he lost focus,** he couldn't conquer Delilah.
- When **Peter had focus**, he could preach on the Day of Pentecost and 3,000 people were transformed. But when his **focus was broken**, he couldn't admit he was a disciple of Christ to a little maid.
- **Broken focus** prevented the children of Israel from going into the Promised Land for forty years. They focused on the giants and walled cities which caused them to turn away from their goal. The giants **BROKE THEIR FOCUS.**

If you remain focused, you can reach your destiny.

Your focus will cause you to live by your vision or the consequences of your doubt. You've got to keep the goal in view if you will ever reach your destiny and purpose. I realize I have used many biblical characters in this devotional, but I must give one more to drive this point all the way home.

AN ALL-TIME EXAMPLE OF FOCUS

In Luke chapter 4, we see Jesus being tempted by Satan, who was constantly trying to break His focus. Jesus' focus kept him on track with His purpose. Hebrews 4:15 says that Jesus faced all the distractions we do, yet he did not get sidetracked. He did not allow His focus to be broken. If you have ever faced temptation and failed, something distracted you and you lost your focus.

In Luke 4:1-3, Satan tried to get Jesus to DOUBT. Again, Jesus refused to focus on the doubt. Many times we focus on what is coming against us MORE than where we're going. Jesus focused on His purpose and His goal. As a result, everything that came into His life that tried to break His focus, He would repel it. He didn't argue or reason with distraction, he just focused. Was it difficult? My guess – YES! He knew His assignment and overcame every obstacle and distraction that came against Him.

2

Broken Focus

Someone who is reading this needs to realize that a circumstance, event or person has distracted them. Know that your potential is yet to be realized. As you read this devotional you have the choice to receive truth and the result will be regaining your focus!

3 Enemies to Your Focus

The last devotional was on Broken Focus. I talked about the importance of focus in our life, home and career. It keeps us on track, determined and energized. When we focus, we continue to have clear vision for the future. When focus is broken, it stops momentum and we see everything through dull, blurred eyes.

This devotional is about three main enemies to your focus:

ENEMY #1 — DISTRACTIONS

A distraction is designed to get your attention and divert your attention. The longer you look at something, the quicker your mind will justify moving toward it. Your eyes move off of what you are supposed to be focusing on and then, accidents take place. "..taking every thought captive to the obedience of Christ." (2Corinthians 10:5 NASB) Those thoughts left unchecked can break your focus. They're distractions.

3 Enemies to Your Focus

ENEMY #2 — DEFENSIVENESS

Defensiveness always comes when you feel intimidated. You loose your focus simply because you start putting all the energy into defending your position. Not only does defensiveness destroy your focus, it will destroy your hearing. Hearing is one of the five senses you have and you need it to stay focused. If you are going to stay focused, you must decide to not be defensive by not allowing the opinion of others to stop you.

ENEMY #3 — PREFERENCE

Preference is an opinion; something different than the original plan. An opinion is something put in front of you to give you an alternative. An alternative will always be a wrong substitute for following the original instructions. That's broken focus. When the highway department blocks a main road, they give you an alternative. It means it's not the original. Your route and plan are being altered; the focus or route you originally had is broken.

- After Fred Astaire's first screen test in 1933, the memo from his testing director at MGM said, *"Can't act! Slightly bald! Can dance a little!"* UNBROKEN FOCUS made Fred Astaire one of Hollywood's best dancers.
- A newspaper editor fired Walt Disney for lack of creativity. Walt also went bankrupt several times before he built Disneyland. UNBROKEN FOCUS kept him determined and today Disney is a household name in most of the world.
- Thomas Edison's teachers said he was too stupid to learn anything. UNBROKEN FOCUS kept him moving toward a bright idea!
- Albert Einstein did not speak until he was 4 years old and didn't read until he was seven. His teacher described him as "mentally slow, adrift forever in his foolish dreams." Again, UNBROKEN FOCUS!

3 Enemies to Your Focus

"And let us not get tired of doing what is right, for after a while we will reap a harvest of blessing if we don't get discouraged and give up."
Galatians 6:9 (TLB)

5/5/19

DON'T GIVE UP!

I WON'T GIVE UP!

What to Do When Setbacks Come

Have you ever had a tremendous victory, experience or vacation and then….you came back to the reality of life? You arrive home to find problems, you hurt your knee running, the plumbing under the sink explodes and on Monday it seems like the entire office has fallen apart! After that incredible high, you come back and it feels like a setback!

I've often wondered why things can change so fast. Moses must have felt the very same way after meeting with God, receiving those awesome 10 commandments and then BAM, a setback! The camp had just fallen apart while he was on top of the mountain!

What are we going to do when life brings us a set of setbacks? How are we going to respond when we come off of a high and into a valley? Can the thing that looks like a setback possibly be something that can work good for us? I believe setbacks can be a **time of reflection** and **learning.** In my feeble strength, my usual reactions to setbacks would include:

What to Do When Setbacks Come

1. **Just ignore them.** I usually try this first. Unfortunately procrastination often makes things worse.
2. **I will delegate them.** Is this really MY problem? If it is, then I have to take responsibility.
3. **Go into denial.** This really isn't a problem. **Unfortunately reality usually sets in and I have to face facts.**

When I get over the initial phase, I usually come to the conclusion that I'm going to have to face my setback head on. That's when these three questions come in handy;

1. **Have I experienced this before?** If so, how did I get through it?
2. **Is there somebody that can help me with this?**
3. **Can I get more information about the problem?**

If the problem is especially tough and answers don't come easily, **the PIP method** can sometimes provide a breakthrough. It's just three little things.

1. **Priority.** Put aside other things and focus on this exclusively.
2. **Ingenuity.** If you have tried common solutions, you may have to think outside the box.
3. **Persistence.** Many times we give up too early. Keep going till you find a solution. I hate doing any kind of plumbing, but I used this principle just the other day and I was victorious!

While setbacks can be painful, they are a part of life. I also have discovered that setbacks can be a defining moment in your life – let them **shape** your destiny instead of **destroy** it! Working through and learning from them is a key component to realizing

What to Do When Setbacks Come

our goals. Apply Romans 8:28 to your setbacks and see what can happen.

> And we know that for those who love God **all things work together for good**, for those who are called according to his purpose.
> Romans 8:28 (ESV) Emphasis added

devo 4

When Someone Messes with Your Plans

Now the birth of Jesus Christ was as follows: After His mother Mary was betrothed to Joseph, before they came together, she was found with child of the Holy Spirit. Then Joseph her husband, being a just man, and not wanting to make her a public example, was minded to put her away secretly. But while he thought about these things, behold, an angel of the Lord appeared to him in a dream, saying, "Joseph, son of David, do not be afraid to take to you Mary your wife, for that which is conceived in her is of the Holy Spirit. And she will bring forth a Son, and you shall call His name Jesus, for He will save His people from their sins." So all this was done that it might be fulfilled which was spoken by the Lord through the prophet, saying: "Behold, the virgin shall be with child, and bear a Son, and they shall call His name Immanuel," which is translated, "God with us." Then Joseph, being aroused from sleep, did as the angel of the Lord commanded him and took to him his wife, and did not know her till she had brought forth her firstborn Son. And he called His name Jesus.

Matthew 1:18-25

Don't you love it when someone messes with "your" plans? We have our life all planned out and then – here comes a curve ball. Let me make 3 observations based upon this Biblical scene:

1. GOD DIDN'T ASK JOSEPH AND MARY - HE TOLD THEM!

I do not note any passage where the angel announcing God's plan asks Mary or Joseph if this is acceptable with them! God simply told them His plan and will for their lives!

> **NOTE**: God has a plan for your life. He made that plan before He created the world and He has no intention of asking your permission to proceed with His plan! You can choose not to obey His will, but you cannot change His will for your life!

2. GOD'S PLAN FOR MARY AND JOSEPH WAS NOT AN EASY ONE.

Sometimes we think that if we are in the will of God, everything will be a bed of roses and life will be without trial or difficulty. That was not the case for Joseph and Mary. **Consider the following:** Why didn't God work it out so the tax was collected either before Joseph and Mary were married, or after the Baby was born? He could have done that, couldn't He? I mean traveling by foot, camel, or donkey, with a woman who was so pregnant that she just barely got to Bethlehem before she had the baby, WOULD NOT HAVE BEEN EASY! I can think of at least ten more instances in just this story alone that made God's will difficult to swallow.

> **NOTE:** We make a terrible error in our concept of Christianity when we believe that God makes life easy when we are in is will and that the easy way is God's way. **When we choose the way that looks the easiest, we aren't necessarily choosing the way that is the will of God!**

3. THOUGH THINGS WERE DIFFICULT, GOD DID BLESS.
They wondered at the child as he grew.

> And Jesus increased in wisdom and stature, and in favor with God and man.
> Luke 2:52

> And Joseph and his mother marveled at the things which were spoken of him.
> Luke 2:33

> **NOTE:** God's plan for our lives isn't always an easy one. But it is a plan that will lead to our being a blessing to many. The truth of it is, when God messes with our plans **IF WE WILL AGREE TO FOLLOW GOD'S PLAN, NO MATTER HOW DIFFICULT, ETERNITY WILL RECORD A FAR REACHING IMPACT FOR GOOD BECAUSE OF IT!**

When Someone Messes with Your Plans

Remember: He probably won't ask you if it's okay and more than likely it may not be easy but, **GOD WILL BLESS** with His plan!

devo 5

Growing
Things
Change!

Did you know that **Change = Growth**? Someone once said, **"When you're through changing, you're through."** God says,

> "For I am the LORD, **I change not."**
> Malachi.3:6 (KJV) Emphasis added

The logical question then seems to be – Who changes if He doesn't change?

> But we all, with open face beholding as in a glass the glory of the Lord, **are changed** into the same image from glory to glory, even as by the Spirit of the Lord.
> 2 Corinthians. 3:18 (KJV) Emphasis added

Growing Things Change!

I believe that change has to be a lifestyle and if we choose to stop the process of life, then we miss some of the best things God has prepared for us.

Here are some change killers. Over the years I have faced some of them. I have seen other people stopped because of them as well -

- **ROUTINE IS DISRUPTED**: habits allow us to do things without much thought (why we have so many of them). Habits are not instincts. They are acquired reactions.
- **FEAR OF THE UNKNOWN**: this means traveling in uncharted waters. Insecurities arise!
- **THE PURPOSE OF CHANGE IS UNCLEAR**: employees resist change when they hear about it second-hand.
- **CHANGE CREATES FEAR OF FAILURE**: the greatest mistake someone can make is to be afraid to make one.
- **REWARDS DON'T MATCH THE EFFORT REQUIRED**: people always weigh the advantage / disadvantage issue in light of personal gain or loss, not organizational gain or loss.
- **LACK OF RESPECT FOR AUTHORITY**: when people don't like the authority who is overseeing the change, their feelings won't allow them to look at the change objectively. People view the change according to the way they view the change agent.
- **CAN'T OVERCOME FEELINGS OF PERSONAL CRITICISM**: can't get past personal attacks and becomes defensive.
- **NOT WILLING TO TAKE PERSONAL LOSS**: any change brings these three things, those who will lose, those who are unaffected, those who will gain.

Growing Things Change!

- **CHANGE REQUIRES ADDITIONAL COMMITMENT**: change usually involves time and when the cost of change is time, many will resist the change.
- **NARROW-MINDEDNESS THWARTS ACCEPTANCE OF NEW IDEAS**: I didn't accept it then, I don't accept it now and I will never accept it!
- **TRADITION:** Cornfield's law says this: *Nothing is ever done until everyone is convinced that it ought to be done, and has been convinced for so long that it is now time to do something else.*
- **THE CHANGE ISN'T SELF-INITIATED**: we want to think of it and not have it imposed upon us.

I'm sure there are many other change killers as well, but these will always stop us if we allow them to stay in our thinking and character. It's been said there are three times when people really change: when they hurt enough they have to change; when they learn enough they want to change; when they receive enough they are able to change.

devo 6

Where's the FEAR?

Today more then ever, when you pick up a newspaper what do you see? You see a good dose of bad news - crime, drugs, violence and murder. This world gives us plenty of opportunity to develop FEAR. Many have been victims of crime. The opportunity to have fear is all around us. Most people have a **fear of Public Speaking**. Believe it or not, this ranks in the top 10 with loss of a job and death of a mate. **FEAR GETS OUR ATTENTION.**

Webster defines fear as a feeling of alarm or disquiet caused by the expectation of danger, pain, disaster, or the like; terror; dread; apprehension, or to be afraid, frightened of or terrified. We are all so very aware of this kind of fear; however the kind of fear I am looking for is "The fear of the Lord." Webster goes on to define this fear as extreme reverence or awe, as toward a supreme power.

Strong's Concordance gives us a definition of fear as **revere.** Webster's dictionary defines revere as **to regard with awe, great**

21

respect or devotion. Synonyms are: **worship, adore, sanctify and idolize.** To FEAR GOD properly we need to have an attitude of REVERENCE, and RESPECT toward God. The proper kind of FEAR of God is to REVERENCE Him and to stand in AWE of Him.

This kind of fear in our daily life, in the workplace and at home would bring an amazing change to our environment. When we do business with his kind of fear, we open the right kind of doors that will bring positive results. Don't take my word for it, look at the following scriptures to see the benefits of the right kind of fear.

The fear of the Lord is the beginning of knowledge!

The fear of the Lord is the beginning of knowledge, but fools despise wisdom and instruction.
Proverbs1:7

The Fear of the Lord is the beginning of wisdom!

The fear of the Lord is the beginning of wisdom; a good understanding have all those who do His commandments.
Psalm 111:10

The fear of the Lord is the beginning of wisdom, And the knowledge of the Holy One is understanding.
Proverbs 9:10

The fear of the Lord is the instruction of wisdom, and before honor is humility.
Proverbs 15:33

Where's the FEAR?

The Fear of the Lord is to hate evil!

The fear of the Lord is to hate evil; Pride and arrogance and the evil way And the perverse mouth I hate.
Proverbs 8:13

The Fear of the Lord prolongs days!

The fear of the Lord prolongs days, but the years of the wicked will be shortened.
Proverbs10:27

The Fear of the Lord is a fountain of life!

The fear of the Lord is a fountain of life, turning a man from the snares of death.
Proverbs14:27

The Fear of the Lord can even help your children.

He who fears the Lord has a secure fortress, and for his children it will be a refuge.
Proverbs14:26

The Fear of the Lord Has Good Results!

Blessed are all who fear the Lord, who walk in his ways. You will eat the fruit of your labor; blessings and prosperity will be yours. Your wife will be like a fruitful vine within your house; your sons will be like olive shoots around your table. Thus is the man blessed who fears the Lord. May the Lord bless you from Zion all the days of your life; may you see the prosperity of Jerusalem, and

Where's the FEAR?

may you live to see your children's children.
Peace be upon Israel.
Psalm 128:1-6 (NIV)

Fearing God Results in Many Blessings:

God hearing our cry (our prayers); prolonged days (long life); riches and honor (prosperity); forgiveness and salvation (eternal life). **God takes pleasure in those who fear him**. Thankfully, we don't **_need_** to tremble and shake in absolute FEAR of God. WHY? Because GOD IS OUR FRIEND! Let's remember that God is LOVE and in love there is no fear.

Let us fear God as we are commanded. Let us fear Him by showing him the proper respect, reverence and honor at all times. The fear of the Lord has good results!

3 Pillars
of Character

Lord, who may abide in Your tabernacle? Who may dwell in Your holy hill? He who walks uprightly, And works righteousness, And speaks the truth in his heart; He who does not backbite with his tongue, Nor does evil to his neighbor, Nor does he take up a reproach against his friend; In whose eyes a vile person is despised, But he honors those who fear the Lord; He who swears to his own hurt and does not change; He who does not put out his money at usury, Nor does he take a bribe against the innocent. He who does these things shall never be moved.
(Psalm 15:1-5)

Pillars are what we put the weight of a building on and are referred to as the support structure and sometimes a cornerstone. Character is something that takes a lifetime to build

3 Pillars of Character

and sustain, yet can be destroyed very quickly. The following three words are pillars that define character for me.

#1 Integrity

- The word integrity comes from the same Latin root as "integer," or whole number. Like a whole number, a person of integrity is **undivided** and **complete**.
- This means that the ethical person acts according to their **beliefs**, not according to expediency.
- They are also **consistent**. There is no difference in the way they makes decisions from situation to situation, their principles don't vary at work or at home, in public or alone.
- Because they must know who they are and what they value, the person of integrity takes time for **self-reflection**, so that the events, crises and seeming necessities of the day do not determine the course of their moral life.
- They stay in **control**. They may be courteous, even charming, but they are never deceitful. They never demean themselves with flattering behavior toward those they think might do them some good. They are trusted because you know who they are and what you see is what you get.
- People without integrity are called **"hypocrites"** or **"two-faced."**

#2 Reliability (Promise-Keeping)

When we make promises or other commitments that create a legitimate basis for another person to rely upon us, we undertake special moral duties. We accept the responsibility of making all reasonable efforts to fulfill our commitments. Because promise keeping is such an important aspect of trustworthiness, it is important to do the following:

26

3 Pillars of Character

- **Avoid <u>bad-faith</u> excuses.** Interpret your promises and honestly. Don't try to rationalize non-compliance.
- **Avoid <u>unwise</u> commitments.** Before making a promise consider carefully whether you are willing and likely to keep it. Think about unknown or future events that could make it difficult, undesirable or impossible. Sometimes, all we can promise is to do our best. Remember if we over promise we will under deliver.
- **Avoid <u>unclear</u> commitments.** Be sure that, when you make a promise, the other person understands what you are committing to do. It would serve you well to ask the person to repeat back to you what they heard you commit to.

#3 Loyalty

Some relationships — husband-wife, employer-employee — create an expectation of allegiance, fidelity and devotion. Loyalty is a responsibility to promote the interests of certain people, organizations or affiliations. This duty goes beyond the normal obligation we all should share in caring for others.

- **Limitations to loyalty.** Loyalty is a tricky thing. Friends, employers, co-workers and others may demand that we rank their interests above ethical considerations. But no one has the right to ask another to sacrifice ethical principles in the name of a special relationship. Indeed, one forfeits a claim of loyalty when he or she asks so high a price for maintaining the relationship.
- **Prioritizing loyalties.** So many individuals and groups make loyalty claims on us that we must rank our loyalty obligations in some rational fashion. For example, it's perfectly reasonable, and ethical, to look out for the interests of our children, parents and spouses even if we have to subordinate our obligations to other children, neighbors or co-workers in doing so.

3 Pillars of Character

- **Safeguarding confidential information.** Loyalty requires us to keep some information confidential. When keeping a secret breaks the law or threatens others, however, we may have a responsibility to "blow the whistle."

- **Avoiding conflicting interests.** Employees and public servants have a duty to make all professional decisions on merit, unhindered by conflicting personal interests. They owe ultimate loyalty to the public.

devo 8

Getting
Into
Position
Part I

"Men are on the stretch for God"
E.M. Bounds

How you position yourself is the key to how you will play. In any sport, position is everything. If you are in the wrong place, you will miss the ball. To be out of position means there will be a lack of score. God wants us to score and score to our highest potential. God desires for us to cross the line as winners, not just casual runners. Why are we in this race anyway, if we don't have reaching the full potential of our God given abilities in our hearts and minds? God wants to make winners and not losers. What's really cool is God takes those who are nothing and makes them winners. (1 Corinthians 1:27) This qualifies all of us!

Today we are flooded with information and are starving for revelation. We can know all the right things, but we then need to get in the right place at the right time for God to use us to the maximum of our potential.

Let me share with you some simple steps I have learned that helped me get into the right position. I don't consider any one of the steps optional and I do believe they are in the proper order for us to get where we are going.

4 KEYS FOR GETTING INTO POSITION AND STAYING IN POSITION:

1. HEAR THE VOICE OF GOD

> "If anyone has ears to hear, let him hear." Then He said to them, "Take heed what you hear. With the same measure you use, it will be measured to you; and to you who hear, more will be given."
> Mark 4:23-24

Look at these verses and the instruction given: *"If anyone has ears to hear, let him hear". "Take heed what you hear".* This is making a statement to us – we need to learn to listen. My wife has been telling me this for years! **"For with the same measure you use, it will be measured to you, and to you who hear, more will be given".**

What we are being instructed here is simple. According to the proportion we listen and hear, that is the proportion we will achieve. Developing an ear to hear from God is so vital in knowing where, when and how to do what He wants us to do.

> **He awakens Me morning by morning, He awakens My ear To hear as the learned. The Lord God has opened My ear; And I was not rebellious, Nor did I turn away.**
> Isaiah 50:4-5 Emphasis added

If he wants to speak to us daily and he wants our ear trained to listen, then there is something He has to say to us. He will and wants to give us daily instruction. Not just instruction when in crisis, but he wants us to know Him and what we are to be doing every day.

2. START WHERE YOU ARE

> For those blessed by Him shall inherit the earth, but those cursed by Him shall be cut off. The steps of a good man are ordered by the LORD, and He delights in his way. Though he fall, he shall not be utterly cast down; for the LORD upholds him with His hand. I have been young, and now am old; yet I have not seen the righteous forsaken, nor his descendants begging bread.
> Psalm 37:22-25

I heard someone say "it's not how hard you fall, it's how high you bounce" and getting back into position that makes the difference. I also heard this statement: "you're like a tea bag – not worth much till you have been through some hot water!"

> He who covers his sins will not prosper, but whoever confesses and forsakes them will have mercy.
> Proverbs 28:13

Start where you are and don't let failure stop you because of what you could have done if you had not failed. Do you have enough to get started? START!

Keys 3 and 4 are in *Getting into Position Part II.*

devo 9

Getting Into Position
Part II

In *Getting into Position Part I*, I shared with you two of the four steps I have learned that helped me get into the right position. How you position yourself is the key to how you will play. In any sport, position is everything. If you are in the wrong place, you will miss the ball. To be out of position means there will be a lack of score. God wants us to score and score to our highest potential. He desires for us to cross the line as winners, not just casual runners. Why are we in this race anyway, if we don't have reaching the full potential of our God given abilities in our hearts and minds? God wants to make winners and not losers. What's really cool is God takes those who are nothing and makes them winners. (1 Corinthians 1:27) This qualifies all of us!

In this devotional, I share with you the last two steps. I don't consider any one of the steps optional and I do believe they are in the proper order for us to get where we are going.

Getting Into Position Part II

3. KNOW YOUR PART AND DO IT

> from whom the whole body, joined and knit together by what **every joint supplies**, according to the effective working by which **every part does its share,** causes growth of the body for the edifying of itself in love.
> Ephesians 4:16 Emphasis added

Knowing your individual part is such a key. You must realize that for you to reach your potential, you play a part in others' lives and they play a part in yours. Again, getting into position will determine how the team plays. If you are in place and your teammates are in place - we have all heard the coach - we have gotten up and brushed off our failure, then we are ready to finish the game. I'm not going to strive to get into someone else's position because it will only slow down the process and hinder the effectiveness of the entire team.

Your part determines how someone else will do his or her part. You are the best person to do what God called you to do. So start with what you have and get into position.

> If you wait for perfect conditions, you will never get anything done.
> Ecclesiastes 11:4 (TLB)

4. GET VULNERABLE – TAKE A RISK

We must move out of our comfort zone. You will find that the closer you get to being in the position you were created for, the more conflicts will come and all kinds of distractions will begin occurring. Why? Taking a risk puts us in the position of total reliance on God. It puts us in a place of expectation.

I have always said that HE WHO EXPECTS NOTHING SHALL NEVER BE DISAPPOINTED. This is so true when it comes to taking a risk. Charles Spurgeon put it this way:

Getting Into Position Part II

"Brethren, be great believers. Little faith will bring your souls to heaven, but great faith will bring heaven to your souls!" So get out there and get yourself in a position where it's God and only God!

There are really only two positions in relationship with how we walk with God: RESIST or RECEIVE. Stay focused, stay receptive and get into position.

devo 10

The Leader's Heart

The heart is incredibly important, but it's not just our physical heart that is important. Especially as leaders, our spiritual heart is equally important. It is just as important to the life of our organizations as our physical heart is to the life of our body. When it doesn't function well, it too, has an impact.

> Above all else, guard your heart, for it is the wellspring of life.
> Proverbs 4:23 (NIV)

As leaders, we often believe it is our experience, our knowledge, or our skills that are the most important component of our leadership. Not so. In admonishing his son, Solomon says that the heart *above all* is the most important. It should be our first priority. Why? Because it is *"the wellspring of life."* Everything else flows out of it.

The Leader's Heart

But what is the heart to which Solomon refers? The Bible uses the word almost one thousand times. For example, just in the Gospel of Matthew we find these words:

> Blessed are the pure in **heart** for they shall see God.
> Matthew 5:8 Emphasis added

> For where your treasure is, there your **heart** will be also.
> Matthew 6:21 Emphasis added

> A good man out of the good treasure of his **heart** brings forth good things, and an evil man out of the evil treasure brings forth evil things.
> Matthew 12:35 Emphasis added

> But those things which proceed out of the mouth come from the **heart**, and they defile a man.
> Matthew 15:18 Emphasis added

> Jesus said to him, "You shall love the LORD your God with all your **heart**, with all your soul, and with all your mind."
> Matthew 22:37 Emphasis added

Based on these and numerous other verses, we can see that the heart is *your authentic self*—the core of your being. It is that part of you that makes you, YOU! It is your inner being where your dreams, your desires, and your passions live. It is that part of you that connects with God and other people.

It is also the most important leadership tool you have.

The Leader's Heart

Physically, your heart is what keeps your body alive. It pumps blood through almost 100,000 miles of arteries, veins, and capillaries. It brings life-giving nutrients to every cell and fiber of your being. Your body can survive without many organs which are important but not essential. However, it cannot survive without a heart. When your heart stops functioning, you die.

Spiritually, your heart is what keeps your organization alive. As a leader, you pump *possibility* into every person and every project. Possibility is what keeps the organization alive. Your organization can survive without your experience, your knowledge, or your skills. They, too, are important but not essential. However, your organization cannot survive without your heart. When it stops functioning, your organization begins to die.

The most important thing you can do as a leader is to keep your heart open. What do I mean? Think of it this way.

When your heart is closed:

> You are distant and aloof.
> You don't connect to people.
> Communication shuts down.
> You leave people to fend for themselves.
> You focus on what people are doing wrong.
> You are critical and demanding.
> People feel oppressed.

The result? Possibility dries up and the organization begins to die.

Conversely, when your heart is open:

> You are fully present and accessible.
> You connect with people.
> Communication is wide open.

The Leader's Heart

You are a resource for your people.
You may focus on what is missing, but not on who is wrong.
You are affirming and encouraging.
People feel free.

The result? Possibility flows through the organization and the organization grows and develops.

The bottom line is this: **it matters if your heart is open or closed**. It will have a tangible impact on your organization. The good news is that you *can* open your heart. This is the leader's most important work. It is foundational to building a healthy organization.

The key is two-fold: ***awareness*** and ***discipline***. With regard to the first, you must learn to discern the condition of your own heart. Is it open? Is it closed? Or is it somewhere in between?

Ask yourself, *Where is my focus—right now?* Is it in the past, where I am grieving over some loss or regretting the way I handled some situation? Or is it in the future, where I am worried about something that hasn't happened yet. Either way, I am not present to what is happening now.

If I sense that my heart is closed, I have a choice. I can either leave it that way or open it up. This is where ***discipline*** comes into play. I literally make a decision to open my heart, and I mentally visualize doing so. I force myself to think about what is *possible*. I choose to see this situation—these people—from the lens of possibility. As a result, I am fully present, available to the potential that exists in any given situation or relationship.

Maintaining an open heart—pumping possibility through your organization—is the most important thing you can do as a leader. There are other tasks of course, but this is foundational.

devo 11

Guard Your Heart

Your heart is the most important leadership tool you have. It's not your experience, knowledge, or skills, it's your heart that matters most of all.

Back in the mid-1980s, I started my first business. There were four of us as partners and we were going to make a lot of money! Things went very well in the beginning and then a few of the partners began doing things that were not ethical and caused division in the partnership. After two of the partners dropped out, it was left to me and one other man to make the business survive. He eventually bought me out and he ended up taking a loss. We almost lost heart! In fact, it was an assault on our hearts and we had to make a decision to guard our hearts.

However, that experience wouldn't be the last time I experienced an assault on my heart. Being a pastor for many years, I have cataloged many distinct situations where I was ready to quit and throw in the towel. In fact, as I have grown older, the conflict has intensified because I've learned that it's our character that is being challenged in every way to finish any way but well.

This is why, I think, as leaders we must be diligent to guard our hearts. King Solomon said it best:

> **Above all else, guard your heart, for it is the wellspring of life.**
> Proverbs 4:23 (NIV) Emphasis added

This is necessary for at least three reasons:

1. Because your heart is extremely valuable!
We don't guard worthless things, we discard them. I take my garbage to the street every Wednesday night. It is picked up on Thursday morning. It sits on the sidewalk all night, completely unguarded. Why? Because it is worthless. **Not so with your heart.** It is the essence of who you are. It is your authentic self—the *core* of your being. It is where all your dreams, your desires, and your passions live. It is that part of you that connects with God and other people. Just like your physical body, if your heart—your spiritual heart—dies, your leadership dies. This is why Solomon says, *"Above all else."* He doesn't say, *"If you get around to it,"* or *"It would be nice if."* No, he says, make it your top priority.

2. Because your heart is the source of everything you do!
King Solomon says it is the *"wellspring of life."* In other words, it is the source of everything else in your life. Your heart overflows into thoughts, words, and actions. Think of it like this, it's like a spring fed river. If you plug up the spring, you stop the flow of water. If you poison the water, the flow becomes toxic. In either situation, you threaten life downstream. Everything depends on the condition of the spring upstream. Likewise, if your heart

is unhealthy, it has an impact on everything else. It threatens your family, your friends, your ministry, your career and most of all, your legacy. It is, therefore, imperative that you guard it.

3. Because your heart is under constant attack!

When Solomon says to guard your heart, he implies that you are living in a combat zone—one in which there are casualties. Many of us are oblivious to the reality of this war. We have an enemy who is bent on our destruction. He not only opposes God, but he opposes everything that is aligned with God—including us!

In the *New York Times* there was an article recently reporting that, members of the clergy now suffer from obesity, hypertension, and depression at rates higher than most Americans. In the last decade, their use of antidepressants has risen, while their life expectancy has fallen. Many would change jobs if they could! Satan uses all kinds of weapons to attack our heart. For me, these attacks often come in the form of some circumstance that leads to disappointment, discouragement, or even disillusionment. In these situations, the temptation to quit, walk off the field or become offended tries to harden your heart.

This is why, if you and I are going to succeed as leaders and survive as individuals, we must guard our hearts. That little member called "the heart" is more important than you can possibly imagine. If you lose heart, you have lost everything!

devo 12

Let GO of What Makes YOU Stop!
Part I

Examine the word - ***Momentum*** - what a great word for a powerful life.

> Defined: "force or speed of movement; impetus, as of a physical object or course of events: *The car gained momentum going downhill. Her career lost momentum after two unsuccessful films.*"

GOD wants you to let go of whatever makes you stop or, loose your momentum!

HE wants you to GROW, INCREASE, BE MORE THAN YOU ARE TODAY. Examine these scriptures with the word **"Continue"** in them:

> Therefore consider the goodness and severity of God: on those who fell, severity; but toward you, goodness, **if you continue** in His goodness.

Let GO of What Makes YOU Stop! Part I

Romans 11:22 Emphasis added

For as many as are of the works of the law are under the curse; for it is written, "Cursed is everyone **who does not continue** in all things which are written in the book of the law, to do them."
Galatians 3:10 Emphasis added

And you, who once were alienated and enemies in your mind by wicked works, yet now He has reconciled in the body of His flesh through death, to present you holy, and blameless, and above reproach in His sight--**if indeed you continue** in the faith, grounded and steadfast...
Colossians 1:21-23 Emphasis added

Continue earnestly in prayer, being vigilant in it with thanksgiving;
Colossians 4:2 Emphasis added

But you **must continue** in the things which you have learned and been assured of, knowing from whom you have learned them...
2 Timothy 3:14 Emphasis added

The next several devotionals will deal with things that make you stop, or lose your momentum. The scriptures above deal with continuing and that is exactly where the battle comes against us as individuals – to stop us from continuing.

On the next page is a partial list of some of those momentum breakers which can be in our daily lives:

Let GO of What Makes YOU Stop! Part I

MOMENTUM BREAKERS:

Indecision	Wrong Friends	Delay
Complaining	Mistakes	Jealousy
Fear	Un-forgiveness	Impatience
Worry	Procrastination	Aimlessness
Regret	Distractions	Disobedience
Obstacles	Lying	Strife
The Past	Quitting	Misdirection
Alibis	Double-	Conformity
Excuses	mindedness	Dishonesty
Tradition	Hesitation	Ingratitude
Envy	Talking	Security
Criticism	Failures	Luke-warmness

There are 5 Characteristics to momentum:

Single-minded - being able to focus on the task at hand. Not moving around into many distractions.

Unwavering in the pursuit of a goal – this is a relentless drive to keep on going even when the obstacles of life hit hard.

Passion, which knows NO limit – always being passionate about the mission. You eat, drink and breath the thing you have begun.

Boundless vision – when you have a vision, it keeps unfolding to the next level you need to move into.

Committed to excellence – to keep the cycle of momentum going, you keep the excellence in everything you do.

The next three devotionals will deal with the momentum breakers of compromise, offences and procrastination. I know they will help you be one who **JOINS THE BEGINNING WITH THE END!**

AND LET US NOT GET TIRED OF DOING WHAT IS RIGHT, FOR AFTER A WHILE WE WILL REAP A HARVEST OF BLESSING IF WE DO NOT GET DISCOURAGED AND GIVE UP.
Galatians 6:9 (TLB) Emphasis added

devo 13

Let GO
of What Makes
YOU Stop!
Part II

Compromise

I press toward the goal for the prize of the upward
call of God in Christ Jesus.
Philippians 3:14

- **Martin Luther** said: "God created the world out of
  nothing, and as long as we are nothing, He can make
  something out of us."
- **What you worship** determines what you become.
- **The world has rarely seen** what God can do *with*, *for*
  and *through* a man who is completely yielded to Him.

There is something significant that happens when we become
<u>wholly yielded</u> to God.

49

Let GO of What Makes YOU Stop! Part II

For the eyes of the Lord search back and forth
across the whole earth. looking for people whose
hearts are **perfect toward** him, SO THAT HE
CAN SHOW HIS GREAT POWER IN
HELPING THEM!
2 Chronicles 16:9 (TLB) Emphasis added

You're not free until you've been made captive by God's
supreme plan for your life. ONLY those who are bound to Christ
are truly free! **ONE IS** A *WILLFUL SURRENDER* the other is *A
CAPTIVE EXILE.* **COMPROMISE** STOPS YOU FROM
SEEING THE FULL SCOPE:

…that He would grant you, according to the
riches of His glory, to be strengthened with might
through His Spirit in the inner man, that Christ
may dwell in your hearts through faith; that you,
being rooted and grounded in love, may be able to
comprehend with all the saints what is the width
and length and depth and height…
Ephesians.3:16-19

IT'S A MATTER OF CHOICE - I am so grateful that God
created us with a choice. UNTIL YOU ARE TESTED IN YOUR
CHOOSING, YOU AS A CHRISTIAN ARE *A THEORY!* Choice
gives us the option to compromise or go with the plan He has for
our lives. The Apostle Paul stated this:

but I follow after, (his choice) if that I may
capture that for which also I am captured of Christ
Jesus.
Philippians 3:12 (KJV Paraphrased)

Look at these leaders who made choices that led to the second
best for their lives:

Let GO of What Makes YOU Stop! Part II

Some bible examples of compromise:
- **Abraham & Sarah** - Genesis. 16:1-5
  Hagar was the compromise of a promise from God.
- **Joash's compromise** - 2 Kings 13:14-19
  He settled for three won battles instead of five or six.

On the other hand, here is a great example where someone did not compromise:

Joshua – he was a leader THAT DID NOT COMPROMISE: He stood his ground in the time of controversy. Joshua 24:14-15

Don't be a leader who settles for the second best of your potential. Be the one who really goes after it all. Be the one who is the best on the job. You can be a person who does not compromise! Don't settle for less than the very best for your life. Open your eyes and see what it is that God is saying to you, and then throw out compromise. You will no longer be a theory but a living testimony.

devo 14

Let GO of What Makes YOU Stop!
Part III

Offences

Part I of this series dealt with **MOMENTUM**, how it works in our lives and with momentum breakers. A reminder of the many momentum breakers we deal with:

Indecision	Wrong Friends	Delay
Complaining	Mistakes	Jealousy
Fear	Un-forgiveness	Impatience
Worry	Procrastination	Aimlessness
Regret	Distractions	Disobedience
Obstacles	Lying	Strife
The Past	Quitting	Misdirection
Alibis	Double-	Conformity
Excuses	mindedness	Dishonesty
Tradition	Hesitation	Ingratitude
Envy	Talking	Security
Criticism	Failures	Luke-warmness

Let GO of What Makes YOU Stop! Part III

Part II dealt with "Letting go of **COMPROMISE**". Today - **"OFFENCES"**.

Do you let things STICK to you? I have been amazed over the years how many people I have met that have allowed something to STICK to them. **For instance:** a critical statement made by a third grade teacher; comments from a negative neighbor; a mistake made 15 years ago or something done to them yesterday; something from a leader or an authority figure in their life. It's a foolish man that adheres to everything he hears. Not everyone has a right to speak into your life.

If you want to keep MOMENTUM in your life, one of the keys is **not letting things stick to you**. One of the greatest benefits of asking FORGIVENESS from God is it prevents things from STICKING to us.

> If we confess our sins, he is faithful and just to forgive us our sins and to cleanse us from all unrighteousness.
> I John 1:9

GOD IS A PRO AT GETTING YOU OUT OF STICKY SITUATIONS! Attach yourself to Gods forgiveness, plan and word then watch yourself become loosed from STICKY situations. The word offence comes from the Greek word *skandalon* meaning a trap-stick (bent sapling), i.e. snare or cause of displeasure or sin. Check out these scriptures:

> Woe to the world because of offenses! For offenses must come, but woe to that man by whom the offense comes!
> Matthew 18:7

Let GO of What Makes YOU Stop! Part III

If your hand or foot causes you to sin, cut it off and cast it from you. It is better for you to enter into life lame or maimed, rather than having two hands or two feet, to be cast into the everlasting fire. And if your eye causes you to sin, pluck it out and cast it from you. It is better for you to enter into life with one eye, rather than having two eyes, to be cast into hell fire.
Matthew 18:8-9

... note those who cause divisions and offenses, contrary to the doctrine which you learned, and avoid them. For those who are such do not serve our Lord Jesus Christ, but their own belly, and by smooth words and flattering speech deceive the hearts of the simple.
Romans 16:17-18

Most people know that we are instructed to NOT create offences. We don't intentionally go out and think "I'm going to offend someone today." But I'm not sure most people know the value of letting go of offences and why we need to let them go! When you really understand the value of something, you go for it.

Here are three top reasons why we should let offences go:

* Offences are a trap to YOU not the other person you are offended at. So, when you know you are being SET UP, get out of the trap!
* Offences are meant to STOP you from becoming everything you can be. In other words, it directly affects your POTENTIAL!

Let GO of What Makes YOU Stop! Part III

• Offences are tools in Satan's hand to make you a loser if you accept the offer of his gift. It's really YOUR choice to take on the offence or let it go!

Living a life where you choose to hold on to your offence and not forgive is like driving a car with the parking brake on. You will lose your momentum and will eventually stop. **A deep-seated offence or grudge eats away at you like a cancer to your mind.** There are few things as pathetic and terrible as watching the person who has harbored a grudge and hatred for many years. Oh please, I encourage you to **unpack** your envies, grudges, jealousies, un-forgiveness and revenge. All it will do is make you become divisive, gossipy and manipulative. The offence will even make you do things you would normally not even entertain doing. Forgiveness saves the expense of anger, saves the high cost of hatred and can save your eternal soul.

AN OFFENCE IS A - **MOMENTUM BREAKER**
FORGIVENESS IS A - **MOMENTUM MAKER**

That you may approve the things that are excellent, that you may be sincere and without offense till the day of Christ,
Philippians 1:10

Let GO of What Makes YOU Stop!

Part IV

Indecision and Procrastination

Have you ever asked yourself this question: **What am I really aiming for?**

Brethren, I do not count myself to have apprehended; but one thing I do, forgetting those things which are behind and reaching forward to those things which are ahead,
Philippians 3:13

One thing I have desired of the Lord, That will I seek: That I may dwell in the house of the Lord All the days of my life, To behold the beauty of the Lord, And to inquire in His temple.
Psalm 27:4

Let GO of What Makes YOU Stop! Part IV

But one thing is needed, and Mary has chosen that good part ...
Luke 10:42

THERE ARE PEOPLE WHO WANT TO BE EVERYWHERE AT ONCE AND THEY GET NOWHERE. The reason is simple ...

No one can serve two masters; for either he will hate the one and love the other, or else he will be loyal to the one and despise the other.
Matthew 6:24

Some people teach that you don't have a choice in where you will end up in the very end. That is deception because your destiny is not a matter of **chance;** it's a matter of **choice!**

Commit your way unto the LORD, trust also in him, and he shall bring it to pass.
Psalm 37:5

To not decide is to decide. Weeds grow easily in the soil of indecision. Get out of the middle of the road! Because of indecision, one can die before one is actually dead. H. A. HOPE SAID: *"Indecision is debilitating; it feeds upon itself; it is, one might say, habit forming. Not only that, but it is contagious; it transmits itself to others"*

Be decisive even if it means you'll sometimes be wrong. *"Don't be like the wheelbarrow-going no further than you are pushed by others.*

PROCRASTINATION *vs. action*

Procrastination is the fertilizer that makes difficulties grow!

Let GO of What Makes YOU Stop! Part IV

- If I don't act now, what will this ultimately cost me?
- Success comes to the man who does today what others were thinking of doing tomorrow.
- All problems become smaller if you don't dodge them, but confront them.
- Procrastinators never have small problems because they always wait till their problems grow up.
- The bible promises no loaves to the loafer.

If you don't do it, you don't really believe it!!!

> If ye know these things, happy are ye if ye do them.
> John 13:17 (KJV)

Your life story is not written with a pen, but with your actions!

> Therefore, to one who knows the right thing to do,
> and does not do it, to him it is sin.
> James 4:17 (NASB)

Momentum doesn't just happen! The common conception is that motivation leads to action, but the reverse is true. Action precedes motivation. *Don't wait to be motivated, take the bull by the horns until you have him screaming for mercy!*

> He who works his land will have abundant food,
> but the one who chases fantasies will have his fill
> of poverty.
> Proverbs 28:19 (NIV)

To the procrastinator**, one of these days is really NONE OF THESE DAYS!**

Let GO of What Makes YOU Stop! Part IV

- WHEN IT COMES TO PRAYER, WHAT HOLDS US BACK? WAITING FOR THINGS TO CHANGE - ONE OF THESE DAYS?
- When it comes to finishing that job, what's holding you back?
- When it comes to forgiving, why are you procrastinating?

What is it in your life that needs to change this year? What are you indecisive about and why are you procrastinating? End the frustration and let go of procrastination and indecision.

If you do what is right, you will reap the rewards!

Are You Protecting Your Marriage?

The way of a guilty man is perverse; but as for the
pure, his work is right
Proverbs 21:8

The media is full of stories dealing with failed marriages.
Most of these stories go on way too long with way too
much information. The truth is, too many marriages are failing
today. We have so many hurting families as a result. The media
exposure has also created one more negative example for our own
children and grandchildren.

You may ask yourself, how does someone in the prime of life,
with a great reputation and potential do something like this?
"How does a Schwarzenegger or a Weiner engage in such
careless behavior?"

It usually begins when someone loses his or her sensitivity
toward right and wrong. We know the opportunities come to

these people day and night thus making then vulnerable. Then there's the entitlement page – I'm special and I deserve this.

The thing that really makes me mad is how society has made this look like the norm. It's in almost every movie and people talk about adultery like it's expected. THE TRUTH: adultery is not normal. It certainly isn't inevitable. It is not the way God created us. We were made for monogamy and fidelity.

When we are loyal, we reflect the faithfulness of our Creator. When we are disloyal, we reflect the betrayal of both Satan and Adam. It is no wonder that the Bible often speaks of sin as "spiritual adultery." Betrayal is the original sin.

However, we live in a fallen world—one that is increasingly indifferent to sexual sin. If we want to live and lead with intention, we can't be naive. We must recognize the temptation adultery poses and protect ourselves accordingly. Nothing will destroy our influence and legacy faster than an affair.

If we are going to avoid becoming casualties, we must have a strategy. Here are three actions you should take in your marriage:

Invest in the relationship with your spouse. It is amazing to me that so many men are willing to invest such enormous spiritual, emotional, and financial resources in relationships other than the one they have. This doesn't make economic sense. If you want your marriage to grow and flourish, you must invest in it. This means investing *time*—dreaming, laughing, listening, and crying together.

Set specific boundaries for yourself. This may sound old-fashioned, perhaps even legalistic. So be it. I think our world could use a little old-fashioned common sense. I've implemented these boundaries into my life:

- I never go out to eat alone with someone of the opposite sex.
- I never travel alone with someone of the opposite sex.

Are You Protecting Your Marriage?

- I will not flirt with someone of the opposite sex.
- I always speak lovingly of my wife and family. I also do this as often as possible.
- I always let the hotel know I am a married Christian man and privileged to stay in their hotel.

I consider what is at stake. What story do I want my grandchildren to tell? How do I want to be remembered? This puts it all in perspective for me. Do I want them to be proud of my life's story or embarrassed? Do I want to be remembered as a person who loved his wife and was faithful to her? Or do I want to be the one who squandered his legacy in a moment of indiscretion?

It is time for real leaders to lead—not only in their professional lives but in their *personal* lives as well. If we can't lead ourselves, we are not qualified to lead others. Character matters. We must take responsibility for our own actions. Our grandchildren are counting on it.

Do You Focus on the Good or the Bad?

He fills my life with good things. My youth is
renewed like the eagle's!
Psalms 103:5 (TLB)

I know there are a lot of bad things out there today, but there are also many good things. Our society focuses more on the bad, no doubt. On a recent trip I was watching a local news report and was shocked with amazement when they started their news report with a five minute "Good News" section. Wasn't expecting it and was completely surprised.

You and I can also be a bearer of bad news or good news. There is so much good happening, imagine if we all just began reporting the good news. Here are some helpful ideas on how to be a good news bearer.

Do You Focus on the Good or the Bad?

- Develop a more positive and productive mindset. Make a goal to find 2 or 3 good things a day. (It can be anything, a story about someone's thoughtfulness, a great song you heard on the radio, or a piece of art your friend showed you.)
- Don't sit back and wait for good things to cross your path but pick up the act of searching for and sharing good things day after day. It's a proven way to better your overall mindset and mood.
- Maintain and grow an already positive and productive mindset. We are all adversely affected by a negative bias; searching for and sharing good things each day helps prevent negativity from taking hold of us. Even more, finding and sharing good things prevents stagnation and promotes growth.
- Inspire, encourage and motivate others by telling them about good things in your life. You will find strength, encouragement, wisdom and humor. You never know when someone will tell you that you made their day.
- Begin writing down the good things in your daily life. Begin posting them on twitter or Facebook and become a voice of good things.
- Keep a journal of good things and at the end of each year go back and look at how much good came into your life.

The good man brings good things out of the good stored up in him, and the evil man brings evil things out of the evil stored up in him.
Matthew 12:35 (NIV)

10 Thoughts That Can Help You Reach Your Potential

Part I

Your potential is something you can be, but not necessarily something you will be. To reach your potential you need to put some effort into adopting these ten points into your life. They do work and you will see greater potential coming from your life as you take them to heart.

1. Never get tired of growing and changing. Get out of the "comfort zone!" Come on; get free from everything that makes you feel safe. Change is good for you even if you don't think so. Also, never feel like you know enough and are good enough and never say "I've arrived". This is a sure recipe to stop right where you are. When you keep paying the price of change, you will never stop learning and growing.

2. Never compare yourself with those around you. If you compare yourself with a dead man, your life looks pretty good.

10 Thoughts That Can Help You
Reach Your Potential Part I

If you compare yourself with a man with no job your job is not too bad. So, be grateful but be careful about comparing yourselves with others (2 Corinthians 10:12). We need to compare ourselves with Jesus Christ who pressed on toward the mark for the prize of the high calling that was set before Him! Remember, wrong comparing can keep you from reaching your potential!

3. Relate with people who are going somewhere! Friends, family, business partners and even church people should not be allowed to keep you from pursuing your dream that is from God and has been confirmed by Him in the mouth of two or three godly witnesses. The bible talks about building each other up and not tearing one another down. We need to be in the fellowship of people of like precious faith, which to me means walking together with those who are in agreement with our potential and purpose.

4. Rely upon the Holy Spirit – not our flesh (strength). Your potential is a dream that God wants to fulfill through you. It can and will be fulfilled only by and through the work of the Holy Spirit within us. So, we must learn to wait upon the Lord. What does that mean? Listen to God and what he has for you and not just what you have for yourself. All of us have our failures, but God wants to bring us into our potential through His promise. Repentance from dead works and faith toward God are elementary principles of the oracles of God (Hebrews 6:1-2) and must be exercised continually for us to move forward in Him.

5. Take a first step. Ah, "Faith!" Faith is an action word. The just shall live by faith. Ours is a faith walk. God may move toward us nine hundred and ninety-nine miles. But, we must go the first mile. We must take the first step toward Him in response

10 Thoughts That Can Help You
Reach Your Potential Part I

to His first step toward us. It is required of us to be aggressive and pro-active in our pursuit of God and our potential in Him.

10 Thoughts That Can Help You Reach Your Potential
Part II

6. Understand victory through hardships. Life is full of tough days and sometimes years! This is where you learn to hide your life in Him! I love the first chapter in James and at the same time I hate it. It all depends on what I am going through at the time I read it! However, we can rejoice always and count it all joy according to James 1:2. We can live knowing that God will not allow us to be tempted beyond what we are able. God will provide a way of escape in His perfect time (1 Corinthians 10:13). God will cause all things to work together for our good (Romans 8:28).

7. Allow others to help you. So many fail at this step. Amazing how we all try at one point or another to be a superman! You will never discover your destiny entirely on your own. God

10 Thoughts That Can Help You
Reach Your Potential Part II

has designed us to live, not only as individuals, but also, in a community of believers. He has given us people, parents, pastors, and others in authority to aid us in defining the meaning and purpose of our lives. To ignore or deny their respective roles could cause us to be less effective or even miss our destiny completely. We must understand that no man is an island. Your potential is intertwined with the destiny of others. The Bible teaches that in the multitude of counselors, there is safety, victory, and success (Proverbs 11:14; 15:22; 24:6).

8. Don't be ignorant. Many people never fulfill their potential simply because they do not know what it looks like. God's people are destroyed for lack of knowledge (Hosea 4:6) and go into exile for lack of understanding (Isaiah 5:13). Learn to read, listen and think. You will greatly enhance your chance of knowing what you should do and could become. The greatest asset to receiving God's plan for our lives is to pray. Asking Him for the answers to life's questions opens to us the doors of understanding, wisdom, discernment, and knowledge.

Some assume that if they do not do something morally wrong, such as lying, stealing, or committing adultery, that they are free to treat the highest destiny of God as an option. However, it is not merely a matter of not doing wrong, but of doing right (James 4:17). If we fear God, we will not only be free from sin, but also find significance in being what God has called us to be.

9. Meditate on the positive. The choice of what you meditate on is yours, not what's around you. What you focus on will propel you or repel you (Proverbs 4:23 and Ephesians 4:23). Don't forfeit your potential by believing a lie (Hebrews 3:19).

10. Don't give up! God requires that we persevere under pressure in order to conform us to the image of His son, Jesus Christ. Unbelief is an enemy of your potential. It will rob you of your incentive and determination to go on. Anybody can quit but quitting is the greatest threat to your potential and blessing. Hold on to God and His words of promise until you walk into your FULL POTENTIAL! (Hebrews 10:36).

4 Key Components to Strategy... According to God

But as it is written: "Eye has not seen, nor ear heard, nor have entered into the heart of man the things which God has prepared for those who love Him."
1 Corinthians 2:9

When Joseph's brothers saw that their father was dead, they said, "Perhaps Joseph will hate us, and may actually repay us for all the evil which we did to him." So they sent messengers to Joseph, saying, "Before your father died he commanded, saying, 'Thus you shall say to Joseph: "I beg you, please forgive the trespass of your brothers and their sin; for they did evil to you."'" Now, please, forgive the trespass of the servants of the God of

your father." And Joseph wept when they spoke to him. Then his brothers also went and fell down before his face, and they said, "Behold, we are your servants." Joseph said to them, "Do not be afraid, for am I in the place of God? **But as for you, you meant evil against me; but God meant it for good, in order to bring it about as it is this day, to save many people alive."**
Genesis 50:15-20 Emphasis added

STRATEGY HAS 4 COMPONENTS:

PURPOSE! Because God is a strategist, purpose is the main goal of what he is doing. He knew from the beginning of time your purpose for being here. You then are EXISTING WITH OUT PURPOSE OR WITH HIS PURPOSE according to which voice you are submitted to. We need to realize that ALL THINGS ARE WITH PURPOSE OR WITHOUT PURPOSE.

DESTINY! Because there is a purpose for everything, a destiny is in his plan for your life. You could say "You are filled with destiny." Your potential has been pre-written in heaven. Isn't that awesome! Before you were in your mother's womb, the bible says that he knew us and all we had the potential of doing on this earth and for eternity.

For whom He foreknew, He also predestined to be conformed to the image of His Son, that He might be the firstborn among many brethren. Moreover whom He predestined, these He also called; whom He called, these He also justified; and whom He justified, these He also glorified.
Romans 8:29-30

76

4 Key Components to Strategy...
According to God

In God's awesome plan for us he also knew there would be things that would come our way, so the next component of God's strategy is ......

CIRCUMSTANCES! Know this; circumstances are always changing in our life and are not a surprise to God. He is never taken back by what comes our way; however, we can be blown around by our emotions and lack of vision for what He is doing! He is the master of dealing with circumstances! We must remember, God is OMNISCIENT (all-knowing). You can allow circumstances to affect your destiny to the positive or the negative. Paul wrote:

> What then shall we say to these things? If God is
> for us, who can be against us?
> Romans 8:31

RESPONSIBILITY! We must take responsibility for our actions which can affect our destiny. Potential means nothing unless it is realized and achieved. We have a choice in the matter. God created us free moral agents and if we are going to reach our destiny, we must take responsibility for what we know, for our choices and for our actions! The bible teaches us that we have been predestined or we have a destiny pre-written for our lives. As soon as we accept Jesus as our Lord and savior, that pre-written plan for our lives gets activated. He called us even when we were sinners and those callings are always over our lives even if we never give our lives to Him. What activates his plan is repentance!

> And we know that all things work together for
> good to them that love God, **to them who are the**
> **called according to his purpose.**
> Romans 8:28 Emphasis added

4 Essential Truths on Friends...

Who you allow into your life is one of the most important decisions you will ever make! Those people will be the ones to influence you, so it is important to choose them wisely and know they are there by God's choosing.

You are the same person today you will be five years from now except for two things: **The people you associate with and the influences you allow in your life.** The bible says –

> He who walks with the wise grows wise, BUT a companion of fools suffers harm.
> Proverbs 13:20 (NIV) Emphasis added

Friends in your life are like PILLARS on a porch
- Sometimes they hold you up
- Sometimes they lean on you
- Sometimes it's just enough to know they are standing by

4 Essential Truths on Friends...

As iron sharpens iron, so a man sharpens the countenance of his friend.
Proverbs 27:17

THE RIGHT KIND OF FRIEND:
*   Will always bring the best out of you.
*   True friends are there for you when they want to be somewhere else.
*   A good friend never gets in your way unless you're on the way down.
*   A good friend walks in when others walk out.
*   A good friend understands your past, believes in your future and accepts you just the way you are.

THE WRONG KIND OF FRIEND:
*   Brings out the worst in you.
*   Absorbs sunshine and radiates gloom.
*   Always seems to drain your energy.
*   Has one person on their mind – themselves.
*   Will leave you for someone better.

Putting confidence in an unreliable man is like chewing with a sore tooth, or trying to run on a broken foot.
Proverbs 25:19 (TLB)

REMEMBER THIS REGARDING FRIENDS:
*   A true friend is someone who knows all about you, but likes you anyway!
*   Surround yourself with good friends and be a better person!

devo 22

INCREDIBLE
Reasons WHY
You Need
TRUST!

One of the funniest parts of **Jay Roach's** film "Meet The Parents" was when the Dad, played by **Robert DeNiro**, was explaining the "circle of trust" to Greg Fokker, the character played by **Ben Stiller**. He explained the importance of the "circle of trust" and how this trust affected the relationships in this family. While we can laugh at the situations of this funny movie, the context of the message is one that is very real and very important.

Trust is very important. Yet, in today's world, ethics and integrity and trust are often overlooked. It is not important any more to do what one says one will do. Integrity is rare to find. Vows are so easily broken they are practically useless. Years ago people didn't need contracts to do what they said they would do. Later, it became necessary to write legal contracts binding people and businesses to do what was right. Today, even the contracts are often not worth the paper they are written on. Courts are

INCREDIBLE Reasons
WHY You Need TRUST!

jammed with civil lawsuits over breaches of trust. Divorces are so easy to get that the constitution of the marriage vow is of little value. Bankruptcies are at an all-time high. Many people's personal credit is a mess because they borrowed and didn't bother to repay. We all place value on trust when our expectations are in someone else, but many don't consider that trust is reciprocal. So, when Dad explained the family "circle of trust" to Fokker, the importance of the trust relationship being one that is unbroken and revolving from person to person was very significant.

If trust is important, but our common sense lets us know that trust is earned and not easily given, how do we survive in today's society in relation to trust? Who do we trust?

> Trust in the Lord, and do good; so shalt thou dwell in the land, and verily thou shalt be fed.
> Psalm 37:3 (KJV)

> Though He slay me, yet will I trust in Him.
> Job 13:15

> O my God, I trust in You; let me not be ashamed, let not my enemies triumph over me.
> Psalm 25:2

> When I am afraid, I will trust in You.
> Psalm 56:3

All of these scriptures were written in troubled times. Things were not good when these God-inspired words were penned. Both Job and David learned that the only person or thing upon which they could place their trust was the one true God, the god of the Bible.

Job, a very rich man, had lost all his possessions, and all his family, except his wife, within a day's time. He then lost his

INCREDIBLE Reasons
WHY You Need TRUST!

health, was very sick and covered with sores. His friends had abandoned him. His wife mocked him. He was living a miserable existence, probably far worse than any of us have or will ever experience on this earth. Yet, through all his troubles, Job came to understand a very important truth. Though he was rich, he learned that he could not trust in his riches, and they could be very easily removed. Though he had a good family, he learned that he could not trust in his family relationships. Though he had a wife, he learned that even those closest to us at times are untrustworthy. Though he had friends, he learned that his friends would betray him. Although he was strong and healthy, he learned that health can be taken away, and he could not trust in his personal strength and health. Everything that we consider valuable in this world, Job had, and Job lost. Yet, the one thing that could not be stripped away was Job's trust in God. He lost his family, wealth, possessions, position, status, friends, and health, but he did not lose his relationship with God. Job understood what we all need to understand. If we put our trust in things of this world, one day they will be gone. But, God will never leave us or forsake us. He didn't forsake Job, and he won't forsake us.

David is known in the Bible as a "friend of God." David recognized that the only one he could trust was God. And, he recognized that as long as he trusted in God, that God would sustain him. That's why, though he feared for his life at times, and was away from everything that most would say was important, David could say things like: *"Trust in the Lord, and do good; so shalt thou dwell in the land, and verily thou shalt be fed."* And, *"O my God, I trust in You; let me not be ashamed, let not mine enemies triumph over me."* And, *"When I am afraid, I will trust in You."*

The Bible is full of stories of faith and trust. I could list many, but the list would be long and you'd tire of reading them. They all have the same theme: God is the only one we can truly trust, that

INCREDIBLE Reasons
WHY You Need TRUST!

if we trust in God nothing else really matters, and that God loves us and will take care of us. God loved you and me so much that his son Jesus died for our sins; he paid the penalty for us, so that we might have a close relationship with the one true God, and that we might inherit eternal life and have life on earth more abundantly.

The "circle of trust" is important. We should try to trust other people, and we should be trustworthy ourselves. God expects us to be trustworthy. Yet, we should also recognize that people will fail us, and we will fail people. If left up to us, the "circle of trust" will at times be broken. Yet, there is one "circle of trust" that is never broken, and that is the trust that we can place in our Heavenly Father. As God told Joshua after the great leader Moses had died, and Joshua was now responsible for some 4 million Israelites who had spent 40 years wandering in the desert:

> Have I not commanded you? Be strong and of good courage; do not be afraid, nor be dismayed, for the Lord your God is with you wherever you go.
> Joshua 1:9

There is one we can always trust, who will never, ever break the "circle of trust." And, that is God.

devo 23

1 STUPID DECISION ... You Don't Want to Make

For the Lord gives wisdom, and from his mouth come knowledge and understanding. He holds victory in store for the upright, he is a shield to those whose walk is blameless, for he guards the course of the just and protects the way of his faithful ones. Then you will understand what is right and just and fair--every good path. For wisdom will enter your heart, and knowledge will be pleasant to your soul. Discretion will protect you, and understanding will guard you. Wisdom will save you from the ways of wicked men, from men whose words are perverse, who leave the straight paths to walk in dark ways, who delight in doing wrong and rejoice in the perverseness of evil, whose paths are crooked and who are devious in their ways.It will s ave you also from the adulteress, from the wayward wife with her seductive words, who has left the partner of her youth and ignored the covenant she made before

1 STUPID DECISION ...
You Don't Want to Make

God. For her house leads down to death and her paths to the spirits of the dead. None who go to her return or attain the paths of life. Thus you will walk in the ways of good men and keep to the paths of the righteous.
Proverbs 2:6-20 (NIV)

Chris was in the prime of his career with a wife and three beautiful children 4, 8 and 10. Chris had everything going for him and life looked like it was just perfect with no problems on the horizon.

One day, Chris was on a business trip and found himself in a compromising situation. One thing led to another and after all was said and done, Chris woke up the next morning in a strange bed not remembering what had happened the night before. Stumbling into the bathroom he saw written on the mirror in lipstick "Welcome to the world of AIDS."

Yes, Chris had a one-night stand with someone who had AIDS and as a result, he too became HIV positive. His wife was devastated, filed for divorce and the family has never been the same.

I doubt that Chris woke up one morning and thought, "You know, I think I'll have a one-night stand with someone when I am out of town. It will be fun and I will never be found out. But then I'll get AIDS. My wife will divorce me and my sons will spend the rest of their lives trying to forgive me."

No, we never have that kind of clarity at the beginning. Instead, we make some small decision. Perhaps for Chris, it was simply a choice to flirt with an attractive waitress just for fun. Then it snowballed from there.

One bad decision became two. Two became three. And eventually it cascaded into a tragic, unexpected end. Twenty years from now, his family and friends will still be trying to get

1 STUPID DECISION ...
You Don't Want to Make

over his bad decisions that were made in a fleeting moment of time.

Remember, we never make decisions in a vacuum. Our words and actions will echo into eternity. Somehow, we think our decisions will not affect others. How wrong! What we do affects others, and also another generation. It shapes the lives of those around us. Remember, you never only affect yourself.

> For the LORD gives wisdom; from his mouth
> come knowledge and understanding.
> Proverbs 2:6 (NIV)

What are the 4 lessons for us?

1. **One moment of indiscretion will be remembered forever and can wipe away a lifetime of good deeds.** It's amazing how you can destroy a lifetime of history! Trust is built block by block and easily destroyed in a moment. That's why we need to deal with the roots in our lives that want to take us the wrong way. "But I just did it one time!" Yes, and it destroyed a life of good deeds.

2. **We are all vulnerable to lapses in judgment. If we think we are not, we are setting ourselves up for failure.** "It can never happen to me." The first line of deception is when you think it can never happen to you. Always remember how vulnerable you are. Put the safety nets up and know your weakness.

3. **We need an accountability system of family and friends who will care enough to hold us in check.** Today, we need to have friends who will be honest with us and we need to have guidelines that are effective to fight the battle that everyone faces. Be smart and be wise to what is trying to pull you down.

4. **We need to live our lives on-purpose by getting a vision for eternal things.** When we get a glimpse of eternity, we begin to live our lives in a different way. Things that used to drive us no longer have dominion over us.

Remember, as humans we have the privilege of determining our legacy. We can decide how we want to be remembered. But this is not a single choice; it is a series of choices. It's never too late to change course and make your life count.

8 Contrasts Between Healthy and Unhealthy Relationships
Part I

Only a healthy heart can enter into healthy relationships. Healthy relationships are central to the Christian life.

An unhealthy heart is marked by fear and control. God's love, on the other hand, casts out fear and is marked by openness, trust, and the freedom to give oneself to another.

I will show you eight different contrasts between healthy and unhealthy relationships. Understanding these contrasts can help you see how healthy relationships are supposed to work.

1. Reality vs. Fantasy.

Healthy relationships are based in reality. Each person is aware of his or her own strengths and weaknesses. There is no need to hide or try to fool the other. Each person is also aware of the other's strengths and weaknesses. There is no need to pretend that problems don't exist or to tiptoe around "unmentionable" areas. If a person is weak in an area, he or she accepts it or works on strengthening it.

8 Contrasts Between Healthy and Unhealthy Relationships Part I

Unhealthy relationships, by contrast, are based on fantasy. What could be or should be replaces what is. The unrealistic elements become the focus. The relationship is built on a foundation that isn't really there.

2. Meeting Others' Needs vs. Having My Needs Met.

In a healthy relationship, each person finds joy in sharing in the other person's growth, in playing a role in serving the other. In an unhealthy relationship the focus is on having your needs met. Sad, but many leaders use their followers to help drive their selfish ambition. When the followers become tired or are no longer useful they are cast aside for new and refreshed ones. This selfish dynamic is at the heart of co-dependency. Too many people expect others to meet their needs. It never works. No one can ever meet such expectations. It is only a matter of time until the expectations are not met and the person becomes disappointed and moves on.

3. Friendship vs. Victimization.

A healthy relationship can be described as two good friends, both contributing to becoming better friends. The strongest and most successful relationships (even the most passionate and romantic marriages) have this kind of true friendship at the base. Where this base of true friendship is absent, the relationship is shallow and susceptible to being marked by victimization or the feeling of being used.

4. Sacrifice vs. Demand for Sacrifice.

Few of the magazines that clutter the checkout counters of grocery stores publish articles extolling the joys of sacrifice. But no relationship can grow without it. Unfortunately, many are more accustomed to demanding sacrifice from another person than sacrificing themselves.

8 Contrasts Between Healthy and Unhealthy Relationships Part I

It's one thing to love another when the going is easy. But the character and depth of a relationship is when the going is tough. You see, love requires the surrender of preference and privilege. Nothing strengthens a relationship like sacrifice. It often seems that the greater the sacrifice, the more thorough the death to self, the greater the potential is for a healthy and long-term relationship.

Our relationship with God requires sacrifice. His relationship with us required nothing less than the sacrifice of His Son, Jesus Christ. Building a relationship or restoring one depends on the willingness of both parties to sacrifice for each other.

Points 4-8 are in *8 Contrasts Between Healthy and Unhealthy Relationships Part II*.

8 Contrasts Between Healthy and Unhealthy Relationships
Part II

In the last devotional, I stated that only a healthy heart can enter into healthy relationships. Healthy relationships are central to the Christian life.

An unhealthy heart is marked by fear and control. God's love, on the other hand, casts out fear and is marked by openness, trust, and the freedom to give oneself to another.

I gave you the first four points last time:

1. Reality vs. Fantasy.
2. Meeting Others' Needs vs. Having My Needs Met.
3. Friendship vs. Victimization.
4. Sacrifice vs. Demand for Sacrifice.

Now for points 5-8:

8 Contrasts Between Healthy and Unhealthy Relationships Part II

5. Forgiveness vs. Resentment.

Forgiveness is a miraculous gift between two people. A relationship flourishes when we are willing to forgive past hurts and disappointments. Refusing to forgive is like carrying around a garbage bag full of hurts of the past. Every time someone makes a mistake, we toss it into the bag and carry it with us forever.

There are no garbage bags in healthy relationships. Out of love, people take the hurts and disappointments of the past and burn then up in the flames of forgiveness. What greater gift can we give someone than to set them free from the weight of their mistakes? When we unlock others from a past they cannot correct, we free them to become all they can become, and we free our relationship to become all it can become as well.

6. Security vs. Fear.

Security is a rare commodity in our world. Often people come from such insecure childhoods they can only hope that their adult life will include a relationship with someone who really cares.

> There is no fear in love. But perfect love drives out fear...
> 1 John 4:18 (NIV).

When we shift from trying to use others to satisfy our security needs to trying to meet the security needs of others, we find ourselves in a new dimension. We are focusing on their needs, not ours. We are filling their doubts and fears with the reassurance of our consistent behavior and constant love. We calm their fears by being reliable. We become in a word, loving, other-focused and totally selfless. That is the kind of love that drives out fear and provides genuine security.

8 Contrasts Between Healthy and Unhealthy Relationships Part II

7. Vulnerability vs. Defensiveness.

In a secure environment, a person is free to open up and be vulnerable. It is wonderful to be vulnerable, to do an emotional free fall and have someone there to catch you. That delightful taste of vulnerability enables you to open up even more, discovering more about who you are, and appreciate all the good that God has created in you.

In a relationship characterized by fear, just the opposite happens. There is a need to build up a wall of defensiveness. After all, if you do not protect yourself, you will be violated, robbed of your identity, controlled, or smothered. The dynamics of defensiveness lead to death rather than to life and growth.

8. Honesty vs. Deception.

There is no way to build a lasting, healthy relationship on a foundation of dishonesty. Honesty must be at the core of a healthy relationship; there is no substitute for it. It is fashionable in our day to paper over unpleasant truth. We deceive those we love, rationalizing that keeping secrets is really for their good.

Virtually all addictions are maintained under the cover of some sort of deception that eventually is woven into a vast tapestry of lies and cover-ups. Dishonesty is a very hard habit to break. One of the main functions of a recovery support group is the accountability it provides, holding a person to rigorous truthfulness. Without accountability, trust and the restoration of intimacy in relationships is impossible

1. Review each point and see which side applies to you.
2. Did any person come to mind that might indicate an unhealthy relationship exists?
3. Will you form a strategy to bring about change?

5 Things You Can Do To Change Your Life

Multiply Your Talents

What are you not doing in your life that God is calling you to do? Do you stay busy so you don't have to do what God might be asking of you? Each of us has a mandate on our life to make a difference in this world. Not because we're citizens, but because we're Christians. That difference at its core is not about what we do, but about who we are. I believe we are called to use our gifts to leave this world better than we found it: with more love, more forgiveness, and more hope.

Get Control of Your Schedule

Generally speaking time is your friend. But time is your enemy as long as you keep making excuses why you don't have enough of it to get involved in changing your world. Little things that you never have "time" to do yield the biggest results: a conversation with your neighbor, taking food to a sick friend's

5 Things You Can Do To Change Your Life

family, reading with your child. When we let our "schedules" consistently get the best of us, we do not have impact. We will never get it all done. There will always be plenty to do. There is always more ironing, more cleaning, more phone calls, more business travel, but special moments with your children or opportunities to help someone in need might not come around again.

Find the Passion That You Live and Die For

There is something that God is calling you to do. You know it. You've always known it. You may not know exactly what it is, or what shape it will ultimately take, but it is unique to you and it is why you were put here on this earth. I don't think this passion is just handed to us like a gift. Finding your passion is the single most important ingredient for changing your world. It's like yeast in bread - without it you will have flat, hard dough. Uncovering God's purpose in your life and following it will lead you to the greatest satisfaction there is. When we work out of our God-given passion, we get tired, but not weary. We need rest, but not a change. Many people don't think they need passion. They just work. They've defined God's will as the hardest, worst thing they can think of to do. They complain the whole time. There is not joy in their lives.

Stop Waiting for Your Life to Begin

Find the meaning in today. Don't miss the life that is in front of you. Your attitude determines how much you enjoy your work. If you don't think enough meaning exists in your life, create it. You are on God's agenda now. He has given you meaning and purpose. Celebrate the significance and wonder of life. Don't wait until it hits you over the head. It's already there; embrace it. Look for the extraordinary in the ordinary. Allow yourself to enjoy even the most mundane tasks; even the work that has been given you for the day. If you can't, you are giving your work, a task, or even another person too much control over your life. If you let

98

5 Things You Can Do To Change Your Life

your soul bubble over while you are working or doing something that is unpleasant to you, you are living a fresh-brewed life, and you can't help but change the world. It is changed by your presence and by your complete freedom to live at a place different from where most people live. It is our relationship with God that sets us free.

Learn to Receive Praise

Why are we so afraid of accepting kind words? We deflect them and do anything we can to let them bounce off us rather than take them in. We think it's more spiritual to do that. However, when we receive words of criticism, we take them right to our core. Why do we do that? Do we really believe it is more holy to let critical words into our soul while praise stands outside in the cold? We need to learn to receive the praise we have been given. If you won't allow people to thank you, you will never believe you are making a difference. Say thank you, and receive it. Don't deflect it and act as though it were nothing. Just receive it. Accept it. Give God the praise that was given to you. Hand Him the glory that someone handed to you. Then save it. Put the card in a special place or write the words you were given in your journal. Next time you are feeling discouraged, go to that place and allow God to remind you that He is using you to change your world.

To Contact Phil Stern:
email - philstern@linkmin.org
web: www.linkmin.org
phone: 636-734-7771

Made in the USA
Columbia, SC
28 March 2019